Michael Foley was born in Derry in College, Derry, and Queen's Univer chemistry and an M.Sc. in computer *Ulsterman* from 1970 to 1971, and contributed a regular ... Wrassler' to *Fortnight* magazine throughout the early 1970s. His previous publications include *True Life Love Stories* (Blackstaff, 1976), *The Irish Frog* (Ulsterman Publications, 1978), *The GO Situation* (Blackstaff, 1982), and *The Passion of Jamesie Coyle* (Fortnight Publications, 1984). He is a frequent contributor to numerous journals, including *Poetry Ireland Review,* the *Irish Review, Stand, Krino* and the *London Review of Books*. He currently lives in London, where he lectures in information technology at the University of Westminster. He is married with one daughter.

POEMS

Insomnia

in the afternoon
MICHAEL FOLEY

THE
BLACKSTAFF
PRESS
———
BELFAST

ACKNOWLEDGEMENTS

Some of these poems have previously appeared in *Confounded Language* (Bloodaxe Books), *Encounter, The Faber Book of Blue Verse, Fortnight, Gown Literary Supplement, Honest Ulsterman, Irish Review, Krino, London Review of Books,* 'New Irish Writing' (*Sunday Tribune*), *North, Poetry Ireland Review, Poetry Review, Rhinoceros, Spectator* and *Stand*.

First published in 1994 by
The Blackstaff Press Limited
3 Galway Park, Dundonald, Belfast BT16 0AN, Northern Ireland
with the assistance of
The Arts Council of Northern Ireland

Typeset by Paragon Typesetters, Queensferry, Clwyd

Printed in Ireland by
ColourBooks Limited

A catalogue record for this book
is available from the British Library

ISBN 0-85640-515-9

For Martina and Jane

CONTENTS

V

I

CHICKENSHIT

So you lie there your own sweat a marinade then a stew
Then a spitting-hot fondue.
No use saying it's not the real you.
We are what we do.

Fauve – with a grey life.
Cocksman – true to his wife.
Flâneur – who walks to work.
Dandy – who looks like a clerk.
Jive cat – who's never once been to the States
(Even spurning a trip *at reduced student rates*).
Sex pusher – with puritanical views.
Status hater – excelling at interviews.
Anti-bourgeois – with good house job and clothes.
Anti-poseur – who's all pose
(Those scornful works not what they seem
It's all hot air a *succès de steam*).

We hoodwink the world with our antics
That hide but can't alter the matrix.

Our fate is fixed though still we search for antidotes.
Some are born to get high on the music others to study the sleeve notes.

Though I have seen Alan Bates dance with Zorba on the beach
I think Zorba would find me too suspicious to teach.

Ah what does it profit a man to see through tricks and charm
The magicians with nothing up their sleeves least of all an arm.

Like Tony Curtis chained to Sidney Poitier on his break in
The Defiant Ones
A mean spirit hinders my freedom runs.

Leave at once! Flee! Fly to the States! Wherever you go
You will find the same city and repeat the same no
As we were warned by the subtlest nobody one of the clerks
In the Department of Irrigation at the Ministry of Public Works.

Though not all's been denied.
Someone sleeps at my side.
Can refusal to shout *The Great Yes*
Be redeemed by tenderness?

Sweet sleep soft as moss banks by murmuring brooks
Long and deep as reviews in *The New York Review of Books*
Come and lay your cool hand on the bloodshot eye
Of a typically chickenshit nowhere guy.

INSOMNIA IN THE THROUGH LOUNGE

Tender night veils the compromised city so many are lost
Spent iconoclasts rejoin the rabble ageing comics serve as game
                                                    show hosts

Secession secession the wind sighs crawl into a hole
And squat silent ecstatic repulsive alone

Yes the genie is out not the beast I thought once
It's not rage or despair but INDIFFERENCE

What it demands is withdrawal passivity quietude
Beard me I'll deadeye you *know nothing don't give a shit*

The through lounge for one who explored the abyss
Heroic Colonist of the Void Conquistador of Nothingness

Does the search for truth end on a killerfoam sofa
G & T in one hand remote control in the other

But *The Car Buyer's Guide* takes me back to the stars
Astra Nova Corolla Orion Espace

Darling choose take control drive
You have the belief

My *Assertiveness Training for Women* succeeded at least
(I lie face down nude and they walk on my back in high heels)

Why not a *Space Wagon Turbo* 1800 cc
I'll prostrate myself in the street and let you drive it over me

And they say familiarity kills desire in a man
My cock leaps like a salmon my heart turns to goo

Ah so much we ask Love to be Demon and God
As well as warmth and double glazing for the cold

It can't take the strain but where else can we turn
Till we leave the lair reborn

With fresh hope and trimmed nostril hair
May our vows under double duvets keep us from harm

ABANDONED SITE WITH PORTAKABIN

The mighty enterprise abandoned or left in abeyance
(Money? Unstable earth? Planning permission withdrawn?)
So that now the site resembles us – neither one thing nor the other
The magnificent edifice never built but the wildness long gone.

No one even looks out from the train
At a row of partly-demolished houses giving on partly-cleared ground
Scattered with skips and heaps of rubble crossed by rutted tyre tracks
And a long sagging stretch of corrugated-iron fence
That connects nowhere to nowhere and protects nothing from
                                                    nothing.

Here too it has all come to nothing
– And who would look on more defeat?
We know it too well already do we not?
My own folly – imagining I was one of the elect.
(Oh I was chosen – but the Angel who beckoned
Was the Angel of Ignominy not the Angel of Fate.)

Yet when the world turns away a unique peace can bloom.
The vigorous purple buddleia growing next to the track
And even sprouting horizontally from walls of scarred brick
Toss as defiantly in the breeze as any thoroughbred's mane
While snagged on the top of the barbed wire that tops the
                                            perimeter fence
More exultantly than flags of nations filthy scraps of cloth dance.

7

Glory of consummated indifference! And here the strange replete
heart
A daubed eviscerated Portakabin with jagged smashed panes
And a doorless doorway open to encroaching tall weeds
Crazily tilted to one side like a foundering ship
But nevertheless managing to stay up.

Secure enough for me to hide with a Chinese takeaway
(The poems of Tu Fu or Wang Wei)
To loll and read and dream and watch the lithe weeds sway
(Occasionally copying a salutary maxim onto the wall like Montaigne)
To put decisively away appearance image status glamour
(Face value is the only value in the city of mirrors)
To defy the god of gold and the superstition of busyness
And to linger in the temple of perception the pavilion of joy all day.

A GREY AFTERNOON IN THE PLATEAU YEARS

1

Today's Special – dour cloud on raw air.
Stack, cumulus, over the city in burdened and variegated banks.

Pearl oyster pewter charcoal slate
I love the forty shades of grey.

2

The fortitude and cunning to carve and hold a good niche!
Some are winkled out – most lured by dreams.

Four more of the qualities that distinguish us from the beast
Discontent restlessness whinging and pique.

3

THE DISEASE OF THE PROJECT HAS TAKEN THE CITY
Defenceless in open-plan offices young life succumbs.

Self-starters, self-managers, such initiative we possess.
If the world forgets to torture us we do it to ourselves.

4

While in malls music noodles like gentle brook water
And real water leaps where shining avenues meet.

So many willing smiles in a welcoming restful ambience.
Not to want anything is the worst selfishness.

5

Foley Plaza – grey sky in grimed glass.
Brood on, sullen cirrus. Sulk, indigent light.

Flow, voluptuous dream of the plateau years.
Today I wouldn't know imminence if it crapped in my hat.

6

I'm afraid Michael Foley is not here at this time.
If you wish to leave a message speak after the tone.

The last freedom and refuge – vacancy.
Je suis bourgeois de l'autre monde.

7

Not that I'm trying to sell anyone the contemplative life.
Often things are a bit *samey* everyone seems a *type*.

And the questions. Truth or compassion? Protest or praise?
Have Burton's Wagon Wheels really shrunk or is it just the
                                        diminishment of age?

8

Nothing answers. Above the clouds emptiness. Nothing looks down.
God we shall never find a solution as satisfactory as you again.

Ah my scornful compatriots, much makes us laugh
But it's no joke trying to love it all for its own sake.

9

Though you seem to be reconciled, window tree
Prince of the cul-de-sac and voluptuary of disdain.

Sway in thoroughbred ripples inscrutable shimmies.
You alone stir. No – the clouds move too.

10

Roll in, looming pewter in front of
Payne's Gray on a backdrop of backlit pearl.

Self-starters, I give you a project:
The re-enchantment of the world.

INSOMNIA IN THE AFTERNOON

1

It's fragments of ancient Westerns I have shored against my ruin.
(Like nuke city mutants weird things haunt the derelict brain.)

Glenn Ford to Van Heflin, Glenn riding a train to captivity too
But relaxed, philosophical, stylish: *I bust outa Yuma before.*

2

And still the fanatically grinning blind harmonica man
Plays with unflagging gusto on the Underground steps.
Blows into it, more like, his dance more a lurch.

Cheery childish sign: EX-SERVICE   WOUNDED IN ACTION   GOD BLESS

3

Dark name-plates discreetly glow.
Sheets gently stir on the bulletin board.

Subdued controlled hum – like on board a great ship.
Superb craft and trained crew – going somewhere.

4

It's the time of the project the marketing mix
(Knock on doors tout your wares laugh a lot kiss ass).

Morning. High on an inner wall
The sun placing calm parallelograms of gold . . .

5

Mike you're OK. Make jokes and they'll
Beat your door down. Go back, friends.

It is easy to seem interesting
– But valuable secrets are scarce.

6

It's a spell makes me seem a prince.
Break it and send me home
Cold silent ugly ecstatic alone.

Plop! A frog in dark pond slime: *profound resonance.*

7

Instead the voices clear and strong
Resources Committee agreeing it has to get its skates on.

Fierce and implacable opposition to the hegemony of essence!

Somewhere a broken king jerks off alone.

8

It's a desert so arid they have to rein in.
'What could live here?' Burt questions, aghast.

Lee Marvin ponders, then gravely replies:
'Scorpions . . . *and men tempered like steel.*'

9

Neither radical compassion nor sublime contempt.
Deserted the crag and unburdened the cross.

Kings, generals, presidents, film stars and whores
We are all workers now, we all 'get on with the job'.

10

But my briefcase of folders and memos
Has a book of poems, a novel and a high-fibre lunch.

Echo on, siren roar of the subsidised canteen!
I like to take my secret nourishment alone.

11

In 'the enforced essential privacy of late individualism'
i.e. hunched, with hunted eyes, tensed for a knock.

Every now and then I make it all the way back home.
Welcome to Serenity   Population: One

12

Where you can gaze past the kettle and the single chipped mug
To a view of a great river basin
– A main drainpipe with tributaries on a wall of old stains.

But above that again the roofs. *Look up!*

13

Functional and drab at ground level old buildings blossom on top
Into cupolas, minarets, ramparts, turrets, towers
Fantasies of belief and defiance surviving corrosive dirt.

Everywhere there are symbols of faith for the faltering heart.

14

Though it's not vibrant colour or strong line
Draws the eye back to ordinary clouds.
They rage sometimes . . . mostly they drift.

I'm stupider – but I feel more.

15

By the path of least resistance
To the garden of remembrance . . .

Decaff and a muesli bar. Darkening sky.

Someone else can arm-wrestle the taciturn gods.

16

Old pros learn to lie on the ropes
Taking shots on the arms.

But with no hope of victory why go on?
Brain damage, happily, spares us such thoughts.

17

O frictionless world of perfect spheres!
The iron laws of mathematics once ravished my soul.

Pewter light. Going home time soon.
How would it be to be smart again?

18

To dispute with the masters on how to live
– Crag or Cross, Nietzsche or Christ?

On the long weary silent way home a sign:
Tudor Way leading to Cedar Grove Gleneagles Harmony Heights.

19

Insubstantial vague light unsurprised unappalled
We blow back and forth through the shit storm of the world

Only settling at evening bizarre double life
Event-driven by day couch potatoes at night.

20

A large one – to put fire in the lukewarm innards
And tears in the dried-up eyes.

Drink and be dull again beyond confusion.
We're meant to get thick as we age.

21

But the lady news readers are strong
Calm at the hour of desolation, spared our bodily decay.

I would like to serve one of them humbly
Hand-washing her pants with fanatical care.

22

Again silence. Gold ingots pass the back window
Last train to the north.

Double glazing around us
Our bone china trembling is all we can hear.

23

Sweet Christ, it is time! Return
And show us how to live in our world.

You get tired of disgust and fastidiousness
But it is hard for the infirm to affirm.

24

Christ will never return. Only I know how truly he suffered
How truly he lived the grim fate of a man

Taking even male-pattern alopecia on himself
(*But the hairs of your head are all numbered* – Matthew 10:30).

25

Send me a flawed human Muse marked by life.
I will kneel down and kiss her stretch marks

My eyes closed not in distaste but worship
The living braille traced out by rapt trembling hands.

26

Sweet Muse, give me my great work
Love in the Polluted City

(Later to be a hit musical
Kiss Me Where it Smells).

THE POETRY OF CLOUDS

If you've guile and persistence
(and somewhere to skulk)
you can even wring joy from
the old grey widow-maker, work.

Once I had the ultimate den
– cabinets, carpets, swivel chair, desk
clear view of blue hills, electric
kettle even, though you had to go

down two flights for a fill.
Also I shared with a turd.
But what do you want for two and six?
Old Taoists don't long for impossible things.

I used to love sipping coffee
in my swivel chair, watching the clouds.
Like my colleagues, grey, nondescript
drifting and frayed at the edge . . .

I'd gaze and gaze
mystically vacant and mildly tumescent.
(Good days, there'd be airliners too.
Those big babies really move across the sky!)

I could have been the poet of clouds

– but I even got fed up there.
(That's the catch with oriental sustenance
– five minutes later you're hungry again.)

The old madness of man
faring forth on the bitter sea.
Too often the train trips, the trudging with maps
the pink form for expenses too frequently mine.

'Mr Foley, would you care to step back in . . . ?'
'We'd like to offer you this post. *Will you accept?*'
Grey clouds raced away down a wild sky.
'Yes,' I said. 'Yes I will. Yes.'

II

HEAVEN IS WAITING

There were five of us awkward and overdressed
opposite this funny sign that said:
WAITING IS HELL BUT HEAVEN IS WAITING.
Well it was funny all right – no-hopers
stinking of Limbo and Purgatory
wanting the Heavenly power and glory
half-believing we'd swung it (as if
you could fox *that* Board – one look marked you
typically chickenshit nowhere dross).
Zeros patiently waiting – all but Wright
a big cross baby, plump and bald, with
the clear glowing skin of the pampered-from-birth.
Desultory small talk wasn't for him.
He prowled, snapping, then turned with a snort.

'This is just *stupid*. I'm off for a walk.'

So headstrong! We hoped he'd be caught and shamed.
Perhaps even sent packing. No such luck.
Brass neck goes unpunished in Heaven too.
He got back as a lady (terribly
sweet and sincere, which of course you'd expect)
bustled in to say:
                        'This is the *hardest*
decision we've *ever* made here in Heaven.
We think you've all *so much* to offer and

we're sad there's just *one* post instead of *five*.
However . . .'
                          (eyes down!)
                                    'a recommendation's
been made. Mr Wright, would you care to step
back in?'
            Up he jumped as if to snort
about time, going by with a secret
smile our so-called impartial lady shared.
They were looking for Mr Wright . . . *of course*.

'Thank you *so much* for coming,' she cooed now,
'you're *most welcome* to stay for lunch which it's
widely agreed is . . .'
                          'Heavenly,' I sneered
unsure who to hate most, them or myself
craving more than my earthbound peers – whom I
nevertheless didn't want to see yet.
A short walk first, between Heaven and earth
the gentle breeze cool on my burning face
lifted to watch the disturbed clouds regroup
and once more fail to find expressive form.

HEAVEN

A gaping inductee with Heavenly
Newsletter, Diary and Starter Pack.
The bad years forgotten – Heaven at last.

God harangued us first, waving the diary:
'This volume's attractive and well-bound
For one reason only.' Prolonged silent pause.
'To give you the rules in a form you won't lose.'
We all laughed. God waved it, serious now.
'Those who've been here an eternity may
Think they know it all. *They need it most.'*
More laughter. Slapping the book, he peered round.
'Every community has to have rules
And all members should see they're enforced.'
Long silent pause. *Deeply* serious now.
'We *cannot* pass by on the other side.'

Then the Education, Counselling and
Leisure Chiefs. The Newsletter Editor:
'This is *your* paper. We need *your* support.'
After lunch Personal Mentor meetings.
Mine cried out affably: 'Sit yourself down.
That is, if you can find a space!' Papers
Folders, books and soiled sports gear – we laughed.
'It's free and easy here – *as you can see!*
Now – coffee mugs . . . *ah!'* He talked as he worked.

'It's a lottery, this mentor business.
I've drawn you – and you, for your sins, have *me!*'
Such gruff talk wouldn't fool anyone long.
As sweet a guy as you could find – despite
I Hate People Who Sing in the Morning
Inscribed on the side of his coffee mug.

Then establishment – all Heaven calling
Me *Mike* and giving me to understand
I could go far – even to God's right hand.
('The sky's the limit if your face fits here.')

A personal mentor myself at last.
My downfall – for tweaking an innocent
Nose was the one thing I couldn't resist.
That eagerness! That confident bright face!
'What's all this counselling racket?' he asked.
'Who needs it here?'
                               I came forward grimly
On my chair. 'I'm afraid they're not short of work.'
Letting that sink in, eyes fixed on his face.
'Oh it's all true. Here everyone gets what
They want . . . *the trick is to still want it then.*'
His face worked, then withdrew. *Who is this nut?*
But I was warmed up now. I couldn't stop.
'The more you get the emptier you feel.
So – who's the unhappiest creature here?'
Going closer, whispering, sly . . . *insane.*
'Think who has most . . . the most status . . . *most power.*'

The Great Man, older and tireder up close:
'Why did you come if you hate us so much?'

'Oh . . .' I looked him coolly up and down. 'To
See you in all your glory face to face.'

God rubbed his eyes. 'A Smart Aleck,' he groaned.

'We have to use the gifts you gave.'

                         'All right
Smartass. *Do you want to go back?*'

                         'To *Earth?*'
This wiped the smirk from my face.

                         Abruptly
He leaned close – intimate, scary. '*I do.*'

Now I was the terrified drowning one.
'They *crucified* you last time.'

                       'But it was *real.*'

I clutched at safe old notions. 'We're supposed
To find fulfilment and peace of mind here.'

We could be pissers – but *God* should be sure.

A big hand slammed on the desk top. Not rage.
Mirth. The old cunt was *enjoying himself.*
His whole frame shook in a wild painful laugh.
'Son, I wouldn't know peace of mind if it
Stuck its hand into my shorts and *jerked me off.*'

HEAVEN: BEHIND CLOSED DOORS

The necessary despairing cry of
Great Men everywhere: Hello and goodbye.

'What?' Mary gasps. 'Away *again . . . tonight?*'

God, helpless leader, displays empty palms.
'It's the Newsletter editorial.
For all those who can't see me face to face.
So many can't.'

        'You can say *that* again,'
Mary says, to her imaginary friend.

'Look,' he pleads, 'I'll get away. We'll have
A few drinks.' Voice low now – and hoarse. 'You could
Slip into one of those outfits . . . like you said.'

'And me thinking you liked white,' Mary sighs.

God palms his ancient brow in disbelief.
An eternity of misunderstanding
Can weary even the gladdest heart.
'I *love* you in white. We all know you *suit*
White. It's just . . . sometimes I'd like a *change*.'

'Admit it – you've always been bored with white.'

'No! You're a marvellous Queen of Heaven.
Don't get me wrong.' As though holding in cupped
Hands a new and incredibly delicate
Species, God drops his voice to a whisper.
'It's just you're so . . . *passive* sometimes. You won't
Do anything.' He should stop – but the words
Burst out. 'I'd love you to *sit on my face*.'

No repulsive insect dropped on bare skin
Could have caused Mary such disgust and pain.
'You *created* me,' she howls, 'and got your
Virgin bride and mother all in white, your
Examplar and icon, great at PR.
If you want your face sat on *make a whore*.'

'I don't want a whore,' God shouts. 'I want *you*
To sit on me – *you* . . . of your own free will.
That's what free will's for. The parameters
Only look fixed. They can all be changed.'

'I tried – but it's *not me*,' Mary objects.

'*Massage the parameters!*' God fiercely
Cries, moulding air with a sculptor's caress
His face bright with the passion and love that
Shaped Man in the sixth dawn. Not today though.
There is nothing before him but empty air.
The fervour fades slowly, the hands grow still.

Each is silent, lost in a private dream.

'And I thought you enjoyed it,' Mary grieves.

'Massage them,' God helplessly, feebly sighs.

Mary's grumpy last shot: *'Massage your own.'*

GOD

I need a new project to lift my heart.
Ah men who complain of your loneliness
Who is more alone than I, cut off from
My work when it's done, more detached each day?
I can do nothing for you, complaining men.
Give us substance and form you cry to
The one who has never had either thing
Give us answers to he who knows too much
To answer simply even simple things.
Should a girl pet on her first date?
Should poets teach or join the BBC?
Ask the sharp wind, the bright stars. Don't ask me.
I have little to say – as I have said.
Never lift your superann early.
Always leave a light on to fool thieves.
Though the gift of self-torture was not planned
That of laughter was. Laugh it off, Haunted One
Whose wants vary inversely with needs
The man who is starving less peeved than
The man who has never been sucked off.
How did I dream you up? But there it is.
We can never call our actions back.
Make your peace with life. Build your own small nest
In the tree of disorder and lies, scoff
Whatever grubs and bugs you can find and
Fling your one-note song at the fretful breeze.

Above – the vague wild clouds suffused with light
The purposeless cloud sheep with fine white fleece
But no hearts or brains to torment themselves.
You too yearn to be passive – but you're not.
There is Reason, surviving despite the
Harsh treatment that brought on his terrible
Breakdown. He wandered for days, lost. First he
Sat on cold stone. Then he lay on wet grass.
He thought it was 1650. He was confused.
Now he lies in a side ward, weak lonely
Victim of mood swings and negative thoughts.
Visit him like a sick aunt, bearing gifts
Glossy magazines, chocolates, flowers and fruit
The things sick people don't want or need
And which never helped you in your pain
But whose human foolishness may make him laugh
And see and feel and think with zest again.

TALKING TO GOD ON THE NEW BRIDGE
OVER THE FOYLE

The best you could expect would be an answering machine:
God is attending a seminar on The Management of Change.
But to talk to the Void isn't strange. I've often prayed to stars
The distant, deaf and *non-existent* screen stars:
Marlon, share your deep power with me. Teach me to brood.
Forgive the familiar tone, Lord. I can't believe in a distant God
Who uses us for some higher purpose we can't understand
Transcendental because of a black balaclava, saying:
'This is beyond you. You'll just have to suffer. Tough turd.'
So it's casual thanks for your gifts – for Manhattan, Montmartre
And the new bridge over the Foyle that sings perpetually in the wind
Attracting a film crew in search of 'the positive aspects of Ulster life'.
I feel Godlike myself at the top of the great central span.
All you Prods to the east bank, to Deanfield, Rossbay,
                              Cedar Manor, Dunwood.
Reap your just rewards, My Chosen Ones. This Land is Your Land.
From the Waterfoot Inn to Larne Car Ferry and from Ballygawley
                              to the Giant's Causeway
Business shall flourish with the words of Isaiah on the front of the till
And no waves but in Lisnagelvin Leisure Centre new children's pool.
You Fenians, stay west in Gleneagles, Ashgrove, Baroncourt,
                              Hampstead Park.
Run up your velvet curtains there. Cast off. Lie back.
Propitious winds bear you off forever from the three-foot men
Upstream where the smoke from slacked parlour fires drifts on
                              the town

And 'the boys' fight for liberty – ('Don't do what *they* tell you.
Do what *we* tell you.') Stronger the scouring wind. Sing, bridge,
                                                        and fly
Your own flag – a jazzy red-and-white-striped wind sock that rides
                                                        high in
Untrammelled exultant wind running like beasts major corporations
                                                        use in their ads
The big lithe loping cats and svelte galloping thoroughbreds tossing
                                                        their manes.
Massive underfoot throb – like a great ship. Touch the rail – you
                                                        feel the singing pulse.
Extravagance and hope fill my heart. *Perhaps I won't die in Derry on a*
                                                        rainy day.
Behind me Lough Foyle and the sea, on the east the North on the
                                                        west the South
Where the statutes are frozen in stone but the statues move
And thousands churn fields to mud hoping for visions of
                                                        sweet-natured virgins.
What appears in most fields are new Tudor-style homes.
Pass on, weary traveller. Bright shine the carriage lamps, sweet
                                                        sound the chimes
But they'll bring you contempt and fury framed in wrought-iron
                                                        perms.
Here on wooded banks aluminium-framed picture windows
                                                        catch light
To make the tops of the top nested coffee tables gleam.
Money talks – wheedles, shouts, swears – but affects a sacred hush
                                                        at home.
Inward inward the gaze, blind the windows that stare on each side.
Lord, we're labelled and frozen like rich men's sperm.
Flesh is weak – and the spirit is weaker still.
Needing hard mind soft heart we loll hard of heart soft in the head.
Though we're subtle as Jesuits still when we justify.
Eastern wisdom I call my sloth and quietude.

Let the young curl their lips in contempt and my name
Be struck from the list of candidates for existential sainthood.
Lord, hear my sins. I speak as a weak man among weak men
With a heart like a deep-frozen haggis and a memory like
                              Kurt Waldheim.
I want to live. I want to feel. Hear me. Vouchsafe a sign.
Let me believe and care. Show me the wounds. Unclog my brain.
It's hard to remember here Your Beloved Son was a thinking man
Not the simpering half-gaga passive Sacred Heart on walls
But the fierce intense Jewish intellectual Pasolini showed
Striding up stony paths flinging truths over his shoulder
To willing but thick-headed followers stumbling behind.
Behold – a man who came not to reassure but disturb.
Awake, Fenians and Prods, from the shagpile dream of The Beeches
Heathfield, Summerhill, Meadowbank, Nelson Drive and
                              Foyle Springs.
Come in, Daisy Hill and Mount Pleasant. Do you read me, Dunvale?
Drive if you must but leave your steamed-up cars at the picnic spots
(One at each end, the Fenian side with no rusting chassis
                              dumped yet)
And climb to the high bracing air where great truths are revealed.
Stand above and between, look down, across and then behind
Where the untroubled Foyle spreads out grandly, inexorably.
Button car coats and ponder. The drumbeat is lost on the wind.
The blood thicker than water dissolves in the sea.
At least the vista should inspire you to country-style song:
From the Lovely Hill of Corrody to the Point of Sweet Culmore.
Sing too, new bridge – though not of what's past or passing or
                              to come
Just the one-note song that sometimes you sing so hard in the wind
The newly social-conscious RUC have to come and close you down.
No cars stop. No one comes. Too far for the three-foot men
                              to walk
And too many career paths here for those who want to feel Supreme.

Also it's cold. Your whole face goes numb. Who can linger
                                            on heights?
Alone, you feel more like a crank. Now the traffic grows – *both ways*.
Not a change of heart – change of shift at the chemical plant
Du Pont, just in sight to the east, seven pillars of economic wisdom
Propping up a dour sky. 'How do you find the Yanks anyway?'
'Miserable shower a shitehawks.' Yet the cars pour out eastward
Glad of the work. More leisurely the homecoming line on this side.
A typical day's freight – the sullen, the weary, the compromised.
Just a bridge, not a symbol of hope – though it sings in the wind.

III

YOUTH

In the stories
the rich and successful old clubmen meet
to exchange heroic tales of youth at sea.

My tale will be modern
with ordinary settings and no plot.
No ploy but images . . . the images that haunt.

A girl springs from her chair to the arm of my chair.
'We must get to Paris!' she cries.
A Paris you'll find on no map.

Or the Indian girl at the staff do
great brown eyes fast on mine
as though our mediocre colleagues don't exist.

That turbulent splendour . . . the sari . . . the bare midriff . . .
I too have had my exotic adventures
Lord Jimming it over her there by the wine and cheese.

A modern tale indeed – no action not to speak of plot.
Nothing happened with either girl.
But I *glowed* . . . and they *came to the glow*.

And the way I describe it
the voices . . . the eyes . . .
the old men are struck dumb in the growing dark.

The sun has gone down in the estuary.
All they can see is my glowing cigar.
'Youth,' I sigh fervently. '*Youth*.'

EXOTIC BIRDS

The scouring of foreskins accomplished, all smegma flushed out of
its lair
Gear snugly stowed, hair washed, face shaved and briskly slapped
With *Drakkar Noir* - a girl need fear nothing but fear itself.

Not that these girls are scared. They give a jaunty fingers back
to men.
Choosing drinks, they say *Make mine a stiff one* and laugh.
Lovely, thrilling, provocative stuff. These chicks won't be
chicken . . . eh?

Yet far from slags. They're not crippled - hopeful and giving still.
No bitterness lurks in their young breasts adorned with such taste
(Like the mums in a cereal ad - a pair but not shoved in your face).

The four enter a bar like exotic birds briefly alighting on country
streams.
Which table's the problem. To see and be seen yet repel the
dull crowd.
They pile coats and bags on all sides. Cold stares complete the
defence.

Warm for each other though. Guys catch the eyes of the girls (their
friend's girl)
In glances that burn as the rounds arrive and the anecdotes flow
Interrupting, interpolating, exaggerating, playing for laughs.

But serious too. The young men are *writers*. Correction! They
                                                'write a bit'.
Hence their loudly-voiced outrage, bewilderment, pain and disgust.
The elders they've rubbished so often they rubbish with gusto again.

The girls feed them life. In a wondering hush one describes an assault
As a child, by a brother-in-law. In his own living room, if you please
Wife in the kitchen cooking, Sooty and Sweep on the box.

Harmony and Great Oneness! A mystical merging of selfhood!
Close, intimate and warm, to drink delight of prattle with your peers!
This is surely the nearest to happiness maimed man can get.

Don't they know it, lone zeros on bar stools observing with longing
(God help them) imagining they too could sparkle with wit and
                                                insouciance
Instead of dispelling all magic with clumsy prosaic insistence.

Such magic, to leave for a pee tears the heart. Though this can
                                                swing too.
A girl has to push past a guy, laughing and freely leaning close.
His cool grin is a lie. He has half a brute-on from just brushing
                                                her ass.

More drink and faster! An empty glass comically overturned
Inspires, instead of pique, a *double round*. Wild comic pleading!
Yet everyone drinks it. Then does so again – double ones now
                                                the norm.

They stockpile for the end. All too soon they're the only ones left
                                                in the bar
Harassed by a barman, the landlord, the landlord's wife. Three
                                                wild heads roar
But the girls, at their splendid and sassy best, force them to wait.

Outside to a lurid expressionist sky by Kokoschka or Munch.
No parties – nor do they care. One or other flat will do.
Excitement will come soon. It will. It *must*. Youth demands it be so.

When faltering humans fail their young the Gods themselves
Take youthful form to set the weary earth aglow.
It will happen soon now. If not tonight tomorrow night for sure.

STRICTLY NO READMISSION

I said to myself, like many a one before me:
                    Daddy Cool can play
                    Now his girl's away.
I mean, she had her fling (though that's another story).
Then again it was spring and the perfect night for a whirl.
                    I went down to *Bojangles*
                    Having covered all the angles.
I had cash, car and skins (to protect me as much as the girl)

And shrewd throwaway lines giving glimpses of awesome
                    Experience, knowledge and wit.
                    OK! RIGHT ON! HOT SHIT!
(Now list six surefire ways to bolster *your* enthusiasm.)
I was hyped up to strike, hold attention and close the sale
                    With a healthy slam.
                    (Top salesmen say: *I will. I am.*)
Nothing was overlooked. (If you fail to plan you plan to fail.)

Strictly No Readmission the glass booth warned – but I gave
                    It no thought, passing bouncers
                    And sniggering loungers
To make for a red plastic seat in a lumpy white plaster cave.
Just in time! The headbangers rushed out like zonked superstars
                    And flung long hair and swayed
                    Grimacing blindly as they played
Wild, screechy, soaring solos on imaginary guitars.

I was the only one watching the girls – some with airs and graces
    Some precocious and unruly
    (Like in years gone by yrs. tly.)
And the new type with scary, dead, unnatural yoghurt faces.
But something . . . something was wrong. My act fell apart.
    I felt estranged and queasy.
    Sport fucking's not so easy.
Post-coital sadness can hit you even before you start.

The lying and joking, the wheedling and coaxing, would pall
    Long before I got my way.
    This was Ireland, not LA
And I was no shit-hot marketing man after all.
I'm a home bird, not meant to open new outlets on Mars
    But to praise and ridicule
    From a padded high stool
Like the barmen who spend their nights off in their own bars.

One pretends otherwise. Only a trained observer could tell.
    I talk tough, I kick ass
    I don't go to Mass
But I'm still the school creep who could never do Tarzan's yell.
It's internalised prohibitions that keep us tame.
    Many fear what would happen
    If all of a sudden
They knew there was no God. Nothing but more of the same.

IN THE LAND OF DISDAIN

Bombed tracks . . . we board an ancient bus instead
HOSE BAN TO CONTINUE AS ULSTER SIZZLES
This is the weather
              If it sticks it
                        Aye

Fleshy freckled arms burned red on top root for trove
Like the transparent halfglobe of plastic you shake
To snow tiny red hearts on a glum teddy bear
Still a fabulous buried culture of bad taste thrives

While apparently impregnable cultures die
My sulphurous town of *So What* in the *Land of Disdain*
Where you carefully aspire to nothing and get despised just the
                                                          same
Has now sold its proud soul to the marketing men
Softly walk by sleeping walls where Time echoes unbreached
Twenty years of history-sanctioned hatred and murder
Having driven the communities to opposite sides of the river
No better place to see present and past in an easy blend

Teeming treasure house of absurdities Ulster never lets you down
Everywhere I half expect to meet my young self
With his watchful eyes hunch of timidity and superior smirk
Micky Micky would you recognise your strange son Mike
Who left to pursue a career in Monosyllabic Diminutive Land

Where the guys are Chris and Nick and Dave
And the girls are Sue and Ros and Jan

Why abandon native riches motive lost in the mists of time
Eight million stories in the Naked City don't even know mine

Like the grey remembered hills of adolescence
Still hazy after all these years

Bizarre and unbefitting sun begone
It's the wild raw looming Northern skies I want to see again
The great cloud masses heavy with non-deliverance and pain
Ulster's perpetual NO in Cinemascope above Glenshane
Forty shades of grey not green should be our song

Instead picture windows of bungalows burn with fierce fire
As late sun lays an ingot of gold on the lough
And the names ring out like gold doubloons
The Happy Haddock Snazzy Fashions Tommy's Bar

Smokey charged haze of *The Squealin Pig Bar*
Avid ambivalent glances of women darting swallows under eaves
Pale inscrutable child waiters carried huge orders of spirits
                                             and beer
And a drunken old farmer sidled up in the john
That's a quare boy yeve on ye does she stand when ye wake

Shock of air from a broken pane drew the eye up
In the smashed window white as a priest's ass the moon
Cold uncompromised stars the true mentors of youth

Later I'd jerk my head up at the lousy band
Then turning on the girl a weary aristocrat sneer
Lay my left index finger on my nose

And with my right hand pull down an imaginary toilet chain
Sarky she'd shriek with a wild laughing flail

And seldom has scorn been received so well
We can pay a high price for our snorts of disdain
(It's not only Mafia dons who insist on respect)
But oh Lordy Lordy they're worth every cent
For my time on the lofty crag no regrets
How could threadbare advantage match sublime contempt

All that believe are justified – Acts 13
So a telephone pole insists to those who pass this way

Maybe I'd still have self-esteem and faith if I'd stayed
No Mr SpeedyFoto showed me my fate
When he handed me the roll of white cardboard completely
blank
I recoiled wanting something more real to display with the robes
Airy-fairy student nonsense
Take it he snapped *it'll look fine*

And still on the corners of villages the classic group three youths
Two of them sprawled on a low wall the third on a bike
With his right foot poised on the high pedal
Watching us in the radiant illusion of imminence

Ah yes indeed my young friends
Through the toiling world your messenger is making his way
The catch is he can take twenty years to arrive
And have barely enough strength to gasp this instruction
Submit to contingency empty your heart of desire

Should you leave and evaporate on the wind or stay at home and
petrify

Two classic case studies my old friend and I
This is a journey to visit him in his eyrie of books
From which he sends cuttings like this
CHIP SHOP BRAWL OVER FAKE TAN SLUR ON GIRL JUST BACK FROM CRETE
Annotated in neat script *No one else here seems to find this amusing*
In return I send books fellow oddball recluse
Our lively children have more to say to each other than we do
Yet we have to go on meeting over the years
I to monitor his balding he to count my grey hairs

I had so much hair myself
The girls swore I used lacquer to get my effects
If not lacquer backcombing for sure
Ah bloody don't
          Ye do so

At the thought of the pushing and punching
(And if you were lucky the *wrestling*)
This thinly-covered grey head bows
My grieving soul trembles and can scarcely endure

Macosquin Derrydoragh Aghadowey Killure
On high poles through the heartland the Union Jacks droop
But the sun gilds the kerb stones of red white and blue
And the vile pink of icing on shortcake rings
That McMaster's Home Bakery dishes on pedestals
Lift to an angry but sweet-toothed God

Gravy rings Paris buns chesterbreads apple squares
Every one a madeleine just to see them does the trick
Whisking me back to tea and buns before the last dance
Mr SpeedyFoto grinning crouched rehearsing us for a snap
Then we take the floor again to sway with the shuffling pack
My sweet knob snug in your perfect warm nest

As they finally open the doors
On the beautiful astringencies of the night

Our bus has stopped again of course
The driver simply got down and walked away without a word

Like weary kings burdened with cares
We look out on the heartland ablaze with strange fire
Ripe and deep rich and full poised to fade

Now the charcoal is ready lay on the great steaks
Pull the cork crack the can drink a toast to dead youth

In late light a man walks to the shop at the end of the street
And returns in exemplary anonymous calm
With a pint of milk butter and an Ormo sliced pan
Perhaps even Ulster has its quota of just men

Such tender feelings blossom on a beauteous evening calm and free
My heart even aches for the sorry old bands
Lack of talent age and discos pushing them steadily off the scene
Those who play badly other men's tunes
Also ache when it's over too soon

Retrospective compassion indulgent better than none
Old friend by the sleeping walls temper your scorn

Whatever we imagined we were we weren't it
We had Flaubert's disgust but not his gift

I renounce my bleak crag for the phenomenal world
And at last a new driver arrives we resume

Out of the somnolent village and back on the road

Past a new filling station W.H. Nutt & Son
The great yellow synthetic-fur die not yet cast
But gyrating in the back of the banger ahead

Mr SpeedyFoto Sovereign of the Transitory
Catch the glory as it hovers on the wing

THE FLORIDA ROOM

Ulster in winter wet dirty a wedding not ours
Crushed in steamed-up cars we pass roadblocks diversions new
                                                                                    suburbs
Where strapped to stakes caged in wire mesh
Scrawny trees fight the rawness and lose

Arriving at last in The Florida Room
Is the fruit salad fresh I ask the smooth *maître d'*
Fondly dreaming of Florida's colour and sap
And unwittingly overstepping the mark
No he snarls in bitter fury *it's tinned*

Not a face to forget however strong the cocktails

Like survivors in civilisation's ruins
Some memories haunt these burned out dead brain cells

For by God I could give you the Magnificent Seven yet
(Brad Dexter's the one you won't get)

Not to mention the Palace foyer step by step
A bald female cashier gave you tickets
Reached for by the stump of a cripple approaching crabwise

Snowballs Babycham Bristol Cream vodka and white
Life does not often sparkle is not often sweet

Fuck yese all anyway fuck yese fir cunts
Across the great window go five wrestling men
Four of whom pinion one by a GUESTS ONLY sign

Then young girls running with streamers
Not nymphs to break the bad spell
But accomplices carrying terrible bonds
The bridal car ribbons to tie hands and feet

Snowballs Babycham Bristol Cream vodka and white

But already the time when you know
That whatever you drink you will never be drunk

To be stupefied by what should intoxicate this is our fate

Not despair but indifference lies in wait
The cunning and patient enemy camped outside the gate

O revellers lovers comrades girls
Resist the creeping brain death and remember these things

Like our nights by the black Sacred Heart in your dark living room
Fierce spokes of light blazed from that slashed bleeding heart
Wearing two thirds up a double helix of thorns
And topped off by a cross in a ring of wild flames

Dali under our noses no one noticed *why the flames*

Once again I am wandering home from that room
Almost dawn spirit rampant the body at peace

Neither villains nor the self-appointed guardians of law
Own the pure streets relinquished by burghers at dusk

Kneecapping has never been heard of much less to kneecap in the head

The soul loves its flesh like the bourgeois his home

Your cry and jackknife not in pain but joy

Later nights in my bedsit the palace of plunder
Books ripped off from Book Clubs film posters from walls
A red warning lamp insouciantly snatched from a site

Remember my frightful ironic zest
As I watched your young beauty in tears fly to crush its soft front
On my hard but lightweight modern aluminium breast

I was harsh as a Cossack indulged as a Sultan

Now sobs of humility rack my whole frame
And the words of love spring to my lips
As readily as the F-word then

If you gave it another chance it could be as good for you again
No you say *no I could never feel that way again*

No one steps in the same river twice
(Or exits from Waterloo Station the same way twice)

It was a once only gift like the Ulster light
With its sudden inexplicable glorious half hours of respite

Below us a great river flashing through trees
All around wooded hills if you look up

Why did I never look up before
Because it was never day always kind night

The Northern Ireland Tourist Board is actually right
With what stunning beauty God mocks our plight
Dutch and Danes enjoy the fairways Germans adore the Fermanagh
                                                              lakes
(A hard race to fool it was one of them sussed God was dead)

Such a mixture of complexity and straightforward blows on the head
In the end you can scarcely remember anything much less think
(And this despite cutting back on midweek drink)

Farewell theorems corollaries lemmas of youth
Irrefutable axioms rigorous proof
(Yes once I knew that sort of stuff)

Instead here's a vision in flawed human form
This woman forty plus overweight lined at the eyes on the neck
Beauty marked by the years and by men
Too late or soon child of the primeval time
Before vaccination jabs that don't scar
And the sensitive caring Caesareans below the bikini line

But good marks not of weakness or woe
With her children all reared oafish husband sustained

A heart full but not heavy *don't press for details*

What could she say what could I say to her
The best of the earth cannot be told anyhow
And besides she's dropped off in her chair
At peace by the fake coal fire's gas flame

Ah hush she stirs lips part a strap is down
Auburn hair sweetly mussed shines like copper just cut
It's really henna conditioned grey but we won't harp on that

For honesty without compassion comes at too high a price
Brutal youth hear me out
Any virtue pursued alone becomes a vice

Or to put it more clearly *let me freshen your drink*
Here we slump on the couch with our booze as day goes

Yet if only we were vouchsafed a sign such rejoicing could still arise
Like the wild light over the lough when the storm has passed
Like Barcelona running out of champagne when Franco died

But all that arrives are sandwiches to rouse us from our dream
In turn surfeit and scarcity mock us a hard and soft team

Almost dusk the great estuary hoarding the light
Below us the river impassive and dark
Stranger fish on its banks than in its heart

In the lounge a guest heckles the high distant screen
The old black and white lovers are decorous time is short
Already taximen call names impatient and curt

Swing of arm beer on carpet trousers feet
Dog intay er ye boy ye his desperate shout

WHAT DO YOU THINK?

Superior and scornful
I felt love and need only after you left
... And now that I am becoming stupid
I value intelligence over all.

The sweet song of steel leaving the sheath
And the keen blade exulting in its purposeful arc!

By which I mean sitting at home at the bedroom table doing maths
The brilliant solutions inexorably emerging under my
                              Conway Stewart nib
While the paraffin heater softly fluttered as though it housed a young dove

But also debate and disputation
Vivian Gill's line of filters marking the watches of the night
Under the terrible acid of my scepticism the coin of truth emerging bright.

Intoxicating vertigo of young power!
Vivian you quivering idealist
You had more chance of unhorsing a centaur
When the ardour and eloquence were mine.

What was proved?
              Solved?
                    Won?
                          Nothing's left.

Come down, darkness and fog. Accumulate, rust and silt.
(Current word-of-the-month – *inspissation:*
The process of becoming thick or dense.)

Though perhaps there remains a trace
Of the old consistency and vehemence.
(Do I not contradict myself?
Very well then, I don't contradict myself.)

Certainly harsh judgements continue. Final charge against my
                                                                parents:
Not so much that they worshipped the dismal God of Material
                                                                Comfort
As that this religion seemed to require the suppression of thought.

To be granted the stupendous gift of intelligence
And refuse to apply it to the conundrum of the world
To sit tight with incurious eyes and blank brow
– Surely this would be one of the worst betrayals of life?

IV

THE DEATH OF THE PHARMACIST'S WIFE
after Jean-Paul de Dadelsen

Rising night wind disturbs the old chestnuts and elms.
Branches try to lash trunks, even trees are self–flagellant.
Unappeasable the fury of questions forced to wait years.

In such travail how hard to sleep and harder still to die.
Long the day long the winter and long too the year.
So many long years and yet so fleeting a life!

How temporary the protection of protecting the children!
How vulnerable the mighty carapace of a mansion!
Lord have mercy. How bitter a thing it is to die

When the earth is so rich yet so wondrously light
Carelessly scattering ripe fruit on the wild roads of autumn
Like plump satin throw cushions in the drawing rooms of the grand.

All night she dreams of her days of dominion – the shining
                                                    dispensary
Sober matt mansion, encircling mature gardens, immature children.
Perpetual the comings and goings, activity, ritual, duty, chatter

The movement and noise that fill the years but leave no residue of
                                                    beauty.
Now, husband dead, children departed, how vengeful the return of
                                                    the silence
Mutating horribly in the stairwell and the dark dining room.

61

Deserted the house and garden giving on fields down to a river
Whose calm and apparently motionless water
Silently bears the dark boats of the fishermen at evening.

Now like bait tied to a sinker the body attached to its oxygen tank
While in coarse leaking boots the soul must brave the wet fields
Trying the boggy margin of the waters that must soon be traversed.

Terrible the sudden utter nakedness of the long-swathed soul
And the forced thought of those who have learned never to think.
Emphysema emphysema emphysema sighs the wind

Indifferent to all the magical coercions of Medjugorje, Knock and
                                                            Lourdes
The Holy Novenas, miraculous medals and scrap of the mitten of
                                                        Padre Pio
Who claimed that the habit of asking why was what had ruined the
                                                        modern world.

Is there any difference now between belief and lack of belief?
Bitter void or better place, equal the ignorance of the journey.
Bitter void or better place, equal the deep reluctance to leave.

Sheila, pray for the innocent wives who never dream it can come
                                                            to this
That the terror of the unknown can merge with the shock of
                                                        recognition.
Dying so much resembles living – dependence, tedium, hard work.

Endless endless the long night which struggles to flow
Like a boat stubbornly moored against the dark current's pull.
Relentless the drag and suck of the waters. Still the frayed mooring
                                                            holds.

The wind dies away. Where is the daughter? Has the son not come
                                                    back?
One last sweet commotion! Still only the ticking of the grandfather
                                                    clock
Steady measured hiss of oxygen from the oxygen tank.

No children arrive – but at first light the sparrows commence.
Mocking as gall on parched lips their indifferent babble.
A bitter final crown of thorns their nest of twigs in the eaves.

THE GREAT BOOK
after Jean-Paul de Dadelsen

Carolling birds enhance the confidence at The Irish Management
                                                          Institute.
'There's an air of excitement and challenge in the country today.
               We can be proud of Ireland PLC.
With our new sense of *realism* and a spirit of *responsibility*
We're sure even the *toughest* of fiscal targets can be achieved.'
GALWAY MOTHER OF FIVE WINS MILLION ON STATE LOTTERY
           Remind me to laugh on my day off

When September rain drips in the yard and I ponder my sins
With the last duty-free. 'Well I've had it. *Up to here*,' said she.
               'Suit yourself,' said he.
So she left. But came back. Affording him another superior role
The omniscient and magnanimous forgiver of sins. It felt good
But what right had he to act the wise and benevolent king?
               No one owns – or belongs.

Least of all to themselves. What goes down in the Great Book?
Am I merely my forgetfulness, indifference and sloth, a dirty-eyed
               Couch potato in the through lounge?
Inertia – the great unacknowledged force in human affairs.
Father it's more than five minutes since my last confession.
I have told lies, procrastinated, kissed ass and whined
               Dozed on a sofa with the TV on

When I should have been arguing passionately with the Void.

64

'Love redeems' – and it sniggers like a bourgeois delinquent:
        'Keep believin' it, Shit-for-Brains.'
How it jeers my desire for a God to address on first-name terms
My absurd need to live with a woman who lacerates and scorns.
Ah Woman, you too know the niggard, the dwarf, the poltroon
        In our hearts.

And men leave you for this. Imagine going back to the immutable
                                                young
With our few scraps of knowledge and our transparent tricks.
        Even worse if the tricks worked.
Immortal confident perfect youth, some day your wince will come.
We bloom and fade. Warned, I love beauty touched by the hand
                                                of time
The thickening waist, rounded belly and full upper arms
        That still reach out at night.

Still the potent sperm of Saint Patrick stains the duvets of Erin.
Though where are we flying, lost Children of Lir? Isolation
        And doubt are the ineluctable fate
But old customs sustain us, for instance augury from Guinness dregs.
Rhyme we no longer expect – and now Reason's gone by the board.
We conclude that the interface is not user-friendly.
        After us let the good times roll.

SUNDAYS
after Jules Laforgue

Autumn! Autumn!
Long-expected backlash of the reactionary wind!
Slamming doors, trembling glass, groaning beams, keening eaves
Annual low-season closure for the winter-long Sunday
(Petrifaction not election our fate here on earth)
Heavy velvet curtains drawn against the dying of the leaves.

Though *amour* at least smoulders like the heaps of burned leaves.

Summoned now by the sonorous Cathedral bells
The delicate and inviolable bourgeois girls
Pass the grotto of the dolorous madonna
With fierce conviction instead of sorrow in their virginal eyes.

So imperious their gaze the harshest mockers fall mute.
Like rebellious churl serfs with their tongues cut out
The young toughs by the back door scowl and grunt.

But of course I remain The Polar Bear
(A wayward ice floe brought me south one year)
Immaculately white as a First Communion dress
The Lord High Chancellor of Analysis
(It goes without saying that I don't attend Mass).

But little escapes my ironic survey.
Is that solemn look just intense piety?

Come, my child, you can tell your little secrets to me
An experienced counsellor and personal mentor
(Book ten or more sessions and you get the first free).

No they can never speak out, they have nothing to say.
Their plan is to frown the world into compliance.

Little angels of fire, the world may not oblige
And may prove so intractable you want only to flee.
Out! Out! Out and away to the mutinous elements
To the bitter dark acres of the disconsolate sea
Sharp derisory wind above and the salt waves beneath
(My own essential medication three times a day).

But now the congregation falls to its knees
For approaching the altar rail is Winifred Fay
Whose chaste beauty wrings tears from manly John Charles McDaid
(Oakfield's wooden-standard bearer on Men's Sodality Night).

Ah the fealty and awe we know only to hide
Unrecanting bound martyr flesh dying in flames
And the height of transgression one trembling blind touch.

Devoutly she lifts a sealed face for the body and blood of her Lord.
Brethren, pray that in this life she has her reward.
Pray the Universe cradles her in a star-spangled nest
And the generations of planets breast-feed on request.

For, Winifred, time sullies everything. Few are fulfilled.
Blows bend the proud shoulders, acid eats the fair skin.
Here the hearts and souls of women are swiftly crushed by mean tasks
While their bodies are stricken by osteoporosis and plastic rain hats.

Lord, how shall we break free and when start to live?

Repetition, ritual, sacrifice
– We march with veiled faces towards a communal grave.

If the Ideal were not so angelic . . . more human . . .
But inevitably the eyes turn to Heaven.
Always the way beyond a life is easier to see than the way through.

With shut eyes and bowed head she returns. Come to me!
(No it isn't that. Conquest was never my game.)
I too want to leave our sad hospital earth.
I want to cross the dark threshold, thread the portals of the night.
I want to rend the sacred veil. I want to pass Beyond.

Irremediably disgusted by our brethren
Could we not quit this life together after High Mass
Leave for ever the respectable matrons in ridiculous hats
And the heavy men leaning one knee on white handkerchiefs
                                        carefully spread
Their unfocused eyes vacant, breathing noisily through their
                                        mouths?

A CERTAIN SUNDAY
after Jules Laforgue

Man the bad-ass? No. Nor is woman the featherbrain.
Ah young men who lounge by the arcade machines
You too will bury your tears in a woman's lap some day.
   We're all sons in the end.
It's just Fate that arms us and sets us at odds
Exiled from each other and from ourselves
Blindly calling each other self-centred and blind.
   To each his anodyne.

I like to walk city streets. Baggy clouds. A vague breeze.
Past the cleaners and bank to the Eat-e-Nuff Grill
For a medium kebab and a chip to take home.
   Joyless dinner for one.
Only roof sparrows watch me eat – my dead friends' souls?
The living dead. O weary friends! But am I more alive myself?
I offer them pitta bread. They're insulted. They fly off.
   It seems I never give enough

That I'm self-absorbed and cold – gibes I won't hear for a while.
She left yesterday. (Now we're getting to it, *eh?*)
The livid hurt face and the wildly slammed door.
   The house and I shiver still.
Every room I go into seems to wince – expecting
The tantrum, the glass of gin smashed on the wall.
Yet when the phone rings how they vibrate, the old walls!
   Wrong number. We lapse.

So many chilly autumn evenings still to come.
Ennui, icy eunuch, has lodged in my dreams.
I must act. Let's engage each other, friends.
                    We must live our little lives.
Look – a midge ballet there in the sun's last rays
The year ending, light failing – but none dropping out
All intent on their intricate, hectic and utterly
                    Meaningless dance.

MOON SOLO
after Jules Laforgue

Alone in a vandalised carriage my carcass is jolted and swayed
But my soul pirouettes like Nijinsky, graceful and mad and gay.
Neither rancour nor anxiety to please mar the soul's pure dance.
But now let's recapitulate, my soul.

We loved each other crazily
But broke it off without a word
Accepting this despairingly
As pure Theatre of the Absurd.

Now the moon in a sterile dream, aloof.
The stars pitiless and brilliant as youth.

Sleep, my darling, safe from the lacerating folly
Of becoming a cosmogonist without a theology.

Why do you not understand? her eyes asked
Why do you never understand?

Because I was reared in the town of *So What*
Where universal scorn poisons the mind.

Neither one of us would yield first.
A typically Irish dead end.

But how potent the Void is tonight! The Lethe must be in flood.
Even I, Polar Bear, feel a shiver in the blood.

When the hot gush of youth falters what can sustain us?

Slowly we grind to a halt between stations.
Somewhere a baffled dog howls at the moon.
Even three-legged council-estate dogs are soulful at night.
Even drab railway foliage can don evening dress
A shining crocheted shawl of incredibly fine light stuff
It discreetly and gracefully adjusts.
A whispering magical with imminence – like lips at the ear.

But now it's time to harvest the Irreparable. Autumn is here
And the stars are more numerous than the sands of the beach
Where the holiday crowd watched you bathe.

Ah my occluded cold heart no sun can reach!
How atrociously I behaved
Returning tanned smiles with a furious grimace.

I should have been glad to rub oil on your soft young skin.
(Already I hear myself sighing *If only I'd known* . . .)
Years will pass. Each of us will grow a hard carapace.

We never recognise our happiness till after it's gone.
On the warm sand your body stretched out in the sun.
How many nights will I honour that image in infamous ways?

Now the sites, yards and dumps of urban industrial waste
The giant spools of black cable, cages of gas cylinders
Stacks of drums, bins, skips, Portakabins with huge hieroglyphs
(Everything tends towards obscurity – even graffiti are cryptic now)
SPECIALIST BORED PILING CONTRACTORS MURPHY SEWER MAINTENANCE

Sheds with rust-eaten roofs and silent rows of parked vans
Decrepit factories with drainpipes and black fire-escapes
Yards with dingy back stairs up to cramped offices
Where irrepressible typists adorn shabby walls
With bright postcards of blue skies and humorous signs
Only Robinson Crusoe got it all done by Friday
This in-tray is protected by the Mafia – HANDS OFF!

Thrillingly sinister the shadows cast by industrial shapes.
I can see us there – existential *Film Noir* types
Two tragic doomed fantastically-attractive outcasts.
Meet me at twelve by the old sewage works.

But tonight there is no tragic destiny no rendezvous.
I am on my way back to a single room.

ATTENTION!
You are now entering the sector of convivial autonomous life
The lighted windows in the old baroque apartment blocks I love
Defiantly raising against the night anachronistic profiles
The ramparts cupolas rococo ironwork and high turret rooms
Where a man could seek sanctuary from the pillaging world.

Does the tremor of our passing touch a soul up there?
Hopper's *Night Wind* woman gazed from such a high room
At the tabernacle of space with the pure Host of the moon.

Sterile moon, basilica of silence, efflorescence of the tomb
Complacent monster of serenity, Mother Superior of the night
Deluding beacon of truth to those who wander in doubt
Mirror and Holy Book of the fatalist, Pierrot's baptism font
Freezing Fountain of Lethe where sirens handwash their pants!

And you, O multitudinous stars, you encourage my fears.

You're the gleams in the necklace of ring-pulls
The Void makes from six-packs of export strength.
Never imagine the Void is neutral it's a malevolent force.
It cracks another can, it observes us and gloats:
Be cool, Nipple Prick, Death is the Last Stage of Growth.

My love, wherever you are at this unearthly hour
Take care of yourself at least, take care.

For we can never stay serene and detached like the moon.
All the sophisticated ironists are smirked at in turn.

Ah why did I never fall down at your knees?
Why did you never fall down at my knees?

Aloof and cold the atrocious moon.
Nor will History relent.
It locks us up for life in the padded cell of temperament.

The Irish notion of compromise – agreeing to be nice
To the other guy after he does what you want.

DREAM HOME
after Tristan Corbière

An abandoned former convent on the coast
The wind chasing itself with childish glee
Through a score of apertures
The only really solid piece
The daunting bricked-up window
Where a mad nun jumped.

Catering mostly for lovers now
Or as toilets for city bus-run kids
This property rich in character (useless)
With plenty of scope for development (ruined)
Gets its first paying tenant today
(Rent – to clean up the condoms and excrement).

A provincial Parisian with radical views
And a weird live-in lover – the Muse.
(That's the story at least – there's no proof.)
What savage gust what cruel wind
Blew him off his local boulevards to here?

No one knows. An unsociable type, glimpsed at windows
Or scurrying by on the road
A long way from their usual literary man
The best-selling novelist playing the squire.

Like the two ends o' nothin'.

Like death warmed up.
Some rare duck, the sergeant said, washing his hands.

All he brought was a sleeping bag, records and books.
All he's done is make shelves for his books
Just a lean-to with planks and bricks
– But what splendour when it cohered!

His only companion a cat called Thelonius
After the maestro they play every night
Dreaming bitter-sweet dreams to the dissonant chords.

Later he opens the shutters wide.
The undrinkable black sea heaves and sighs
And the undead ride the wind with the desolate cries
Of unrecognised poets soliciting praise.
Let us in, let us in to the warmth and light.

How even no-hopers cling to their verse
The feet running on long after death
Like a goose with its head chopped off.

Tired of struggling with poetry now
It's a letter he turns back to write:

'I exist here, ghostly, faint, obscure
A wrong line incompletely Tippexed out.

'You were right to erase, Chérie.
Scarcely meant for felicity
My dislikes were the only real part of me.

'While others were staking out their loves
I was hacking away at tumours in surgeon's gloves.

'You can't nurse hatreds here
Where the wind roams the shore like a bored child
Picking at wrack, chasing clouds
Idly bending the wild grasses this way and that.
It's not hate but indifference
Threatens the exiled heart.

'Could I make a fresh start?
Learn to care the right way?

'Oh come back! Be my burden again! *Lumber me!*
Make my ancient Aeolian hinges groan.
Make my freshly-oiled weather cock
Spin in the gale of
Your justified wrath at such *worthlessness*.

'Raise the mad nun from her grave with your blasphemy
Thrusting down fiercely in joy and contempt.

'Afterwards we can walk through my forest of firs
Be alarmed and make jokes at the sinister farm
Where a chainsaw massacre must have occurred.

'Be amused and make jokes
At the poster advertising MONSTER SPORTS
(What events will the monsters have?)

'Then be visually literate and praise
How the cobalt blue of an outhouse
Leaps from the valley's browns and greys.

'Back home for long silent intimacy
My bleak head on your breast, my hands gently astir
Like a light breeze, caressing with sighs

In an exquisite tenderness
Slowly rekindling desire.

'Let the winter bite hard! Let it howl, freeze and pour!
The true spring is the bloom of your fresh twenty-four.
O fragrance of youth gaily cast on the wind!

'And I'll build you a barbecue pit in the spring
Or if you've gone natural
Home-grown fresh veg of the season
I'll lay at your feet – good simple things
And my heart (less so) but wild for you alone

'Wild as these winter squalls lashing the shore.
Stairs, weather cock, shutters . . . the very beams groan.

'I daydream – *You!*
I wet dream – *You!*

'The storm howls your lost name
And the shutters' arms beckon insanely – *You! You!*

'You're everywhere – but vague. Come forth!
A knock.
            You!
                  The mad nun!
                        No – a rat.

'Where we stay becomes our habitat.
Here the last entropic fling begins.
Rats jive in the attic. Slates take to the sky.

'I leave you the best of my jokes.
Laugh if you don't get it. Cry if you do.

All I wanted to be was just folks.'

He opened the shutters wide. It was light.
Tore the letter in bits . . . let them fall.
They fluttered straight down of course
But he fancied the white scraps gulls in flight
Bold, unwearying, poised to swoop
Bearing inland to tower block and semi
Their contumacious cries.

APOLLINAIRE IN DUBLIN

What restlessness what boredoms what futilities O Man
In the age of accelerating obsolescence and contracting attention span

Now even the new models look out of date
And Religion alone comes up fresh giving hope
John Joe Quigley the midfield man profiled today
Under *Character I Would Most Like to Meet*
Gives *His Holiness the Pope*

This is the poetry of the morning press
As for prose
PARENTS USE SON (2) AS HUMAN FOOTBALL

Like a crazy old filthy bagwoman the city stinks and roars

But with perfect clothes hair face accessories matched
Down the scumbag street come the beautiful shorthand typists
                                            unperturbed
If you take enough care with minutiae
The big bad things go away
Cheeriness also helps close your eyes and pretend

The street is really young and you're a boy again yourself
Your mother dresses you in a short-trousered suit
And drags a comb like a harrow across your head
Don't be pullin down your socks or kickin stones with those shoes

You look the part at last and with your old friend John McCabe
You are walking to the college chapel for your twenty minute stint
At the Forty Hours' Adoration of the Sacred Heart
Candle flames like an undulant sea you're lightheaded you're stunned
Yourself tremulous holy and pure
As the flame of a candle lit for a widow's ailing only son

In the centre the blazing glory of Christ exposed
The stong and everflowering tree of all our prayers
Flamehaired torch that no wind can put out
Lovely lily we water with tears

When will he return to teach his people how to live
Unlike him they expire on a Sunday and try to be reborn on
                                        Friday night
With the help of a large gin and tonic (slimline)
A tape of Nice N Easy sounds and soft indirect light
As The National Childbirth Trust advise
No stone is rolled away no corpse comes forth

Now you're walking the streets of Dublin alone among the crowd
Love anxiety seizes your throat
You will never be loved again now you feel sure
Ashamed you catch yourself saying a prayer
Then you laugh at yourself and like a flash of hellfire
The sparks of wild laughter light up the depths of your soul
There an old portrait hangs in a gloomy museum
You go close for a look and draw back appalled

And this was also Christ I hate it the time when beauty failed
Our Lady of Perpetual Suckers intercede for me now

From her grottos and niches the Virgin looks down with
                                        compassionate eyes

But the bourgeois ladies here sweep by like galleons under sail
The proud sail of a full purse
Certainties of comfort and status keeping them regally on course

However often you changed your underwear
And trimmed your nostril hair
These types would give nothing away
Without making you beg and grovel (Irish foreplay)

Yes I would do that have done it love is a shameful disease
One image haunting sleepless nights and aimless days

And now you are back in the happy time
On the Mediterranean shore
As the marvellously sassy sisters shriek with joy in the pedal boats

Then at a table in the sun on the table a vase of flowers
You ought to be salving your conscience you ought to be working
at prose
Instead you watch in a trance the insect asleep in the heart of the rose

Are the hands of the clock by the Green going round the wrong way
You are passing slowly backwards through your life

Here you are alone in your bedsitter wild beast or God

Next a gauche convent school teacher (*Übermensch* where is your
power)

And here kissing ass again in London *next slide please*

So many painful and joyous journeys
Before you discover the truth of the world
Ageing and lies are the truth of the world

Cuntstruck and heartsick at 20 at 35 the same
I have lived like an idiot and wasted my life
I no longer dare to look at my hands and feel like bursting into tears

You must look almost as desperate as these harassed Dublin girls
Double buggy with shopping and one by the hand
A red and workworn hand
With which she savagely slashes the legs of the standing child

These are not evil women they just have their cares
And even the ugliest of them can give her man hell

It's the thought of her youthful scored belly that moves me to
                                                          tears
I could kneel down here in the street and kiss her warm stretch
                                              marks don't laugh

No you don't often laugh my poor angel just as well
Stress incontinence from too many kids makes you pee yourself
                                              when you laugh

Now you're standing at the bar of a low den it's well past time
We must clear de house now Ah come now playse

You are drinking hard liquor that burns down like life
Your life you also gulp neat without mixer or ice

You want to walk away from the guns you want to go home you
                                              want out
You want to drift off to sleep among alien gods
You want to be carried away on a litter by South Sea Island girls

You're like Lazarus appalled by the light
But there's no going back or going home

Night slowly fades like the beauty of women
And at dawn the milk floats come

Brutal triumphant and merciless
Day with the guillotined head of the sun

THE BEAUTIFUL REDHEAD
after Guillaume Apollinaire

Here I stand before you a man apparently of parts
Who has moved around a bit at least among these isles
From the little towns enamoured of their own inertia and sloth
To the attenuated city with its meaningless scope
Just the man to name a victor in the neverending war
Between the choking rich swamp of home and freedom's thin empty air
But I never discovered where to live I just ran out of steam

Ah privileged citizens who have looked on God's face
(Its apparent from your scrupulous imitation of His Mouth)
You who were vouchsafed a sign and strode at once to the
                                        appointed place
Forgive me my ignorance forgive me the waste
Be gentle with those who still wonder and quest
Forever confused as children stunned by the great Pick'n'Mix of
                                        the world

We are not the enemy we want to bring you back trove
Not just gypsy tales of romance
The unplucked flowers of mystery colours and fires never seen
But a strange unexpected gift *tenderness*
A vast and peaceful country almost completely unexplored
Some day we will go with a cooler box arm in arm
But so many things need to be seized and brought back
Pity those in the forward positions
Forgive us our errors forgive us our sins

And now it is summer the violent season
My youth is dead as spring it's late

Still I wait to experience an infinite ardour
Some imperative combining youth's passion and the reason of years
A dream I personify as a beautiful fiery redhead
Rhonda Fleming as Cheyenne O Malley in *Bull Whip*
Get back on that horse before I cut you to shreds

Go on laugh if you like laugh at me go on laugh
You city hard dicks and especially men of the small towns
With universal contempt in your bones
To you there's so much I would not dare reveal
So many things *you* would never let me reveal
Rhonda my vain hope my grief
Pity me

HOMAGE TO LIFE
after Jules Supervielle

Good to have found a secure home
(our defences cunning as well as strong
lights go on and off even when we're out)
to appreciate earth, sun and moon
like domestics one couldn't replace
to sell time a lease on a stable heart
and give the words – wife, child – a face
to hold chaos at bay for a while
controlling the past by forgiveness
controlling the future by pledges
a world that can fit in cupped hands
like an apple on the garden apple tree
not the large world one dreamed but with
room for the spirit and room for the heart
and a spare room for wandering bards
bringing news of the troubadour life.
To store bag and worn guitar case in the hall
to provide meals and answer phone calls
('Not here but should be back soon'
reassurance for numerous anxious girls)
– a small price to have fugitive glory
alight, bards of passage so soon on the wing
bronze heads soon borne off by the feet of clay.
Then to sit in the window seat, near the big tree
and to come upon one's own soul, cautiously
gliding with shipped oars at twilight

so as not to scare the little thing off.
Nor should the flawed faulty body be scorned
though it adds to the ever-increasing
complexity problems of fading powers
(never the time and the place and your love
and a brute-on all together).
Good to sit by the jubilant born-again leaves
and feel age creeping over the naked flesh
at one with the labouring blood in the veins.
Shine down, Star of Patience, on all obscure toil.
And to choose from a head full of words
the least gorgeous, least solemn ones
the handled, soiled, most-despised ones
the world's junk – what joy to retrieve it
and make it shine a moment in poems.

V

THE HAG OF BRÉHEC

Through the loud gross tanned beach crowd
She passed – forty-plus, six foot, lean
Completely grey – but with a look
That struck us dumb, my friend and I
Paralysed there by the sea wall
Books forgotten in our hands.
My old friend recovered first
To mutter in fervent awe:
That woman hasn't signed off at all.

I must have slept. The light is gone.
Family, friends and crowd are gone.
Ditto French bread, cheese and wine.
An empty beach reverts to God.
Small waves break cautiously, fearful
And low. By the rocks – *there!* In
Tracksuit top and bikini pants
Splendid and grim. She beckons me.
All my life I have watched for a sign.
I follow her over the sand
And up the hill, the wind rising
Vindictive and personal now
Hating tourist and native alike.
To stay home and have roots doesn't help.
Chaos and ruin call. Every
Road leads to the grave on the hill

Where she waits, minus top and pants
Knowing I like dissolution's
Marks, grey hair and pallid skin
Cheek grooves like sabre cuts
Actual scars where the scalpel
Slashed, iridescent purple weals
Lurid blooms of the fading light.
She laughs. The wind hollers. Black trees
Wildly thrash their encouragement:
Go with it. Go with the flow.
Join the wild entropic jive. From
The woods, from the sea, from the sky
Disorder calls. Why wait to be
Torn apart – let go and fly.
Face her. Straddle the open grave
As she leaps on, shrieking, long
Grey hair spread out in the wind
Thrusting savagely forward and down.
Shriek yourself, feeling flesh dissolve
Spasm on spasm on spasm on spasm
Flaying your shocked legs to tripe.

ELEGY FOR THELONIUS

No doctor has put his finger on what is wrong with him, and he
has had every medical test under the sun. He's not unhappy, and
his mind works very well. He's withdrawn, that's all.

BARONESS PANNONICA DE KOENIGSWARTER

. . . like your sister trying over sheet music from Woolworth's . . .

PHILIP LARKIN

I went to *Jazz on a Summer's Day*
Just to see Thelonius play
His one number – *Blue Monk* – but
As soon as he started his solo they cut
To a yacht race out in the bay.

Rich college kids easy on ear and eye
Unlike dissonant, vinegary
Monk's halting notes, spikey chords, broken runs.
Weird city – but it stuns.
You wonder what's driving the guy.

There has to be something, this is the catch.
No torrent of notes, no technique, can match
The obsessive insistent way
Of a man with things to say
Grimly fighting his demons' clutch.

Sad defeat in the mansion of Nica de K

Ten years a recluse, piano twenty feet away
Untouched – abandoned for bed and the telly
His Nellie (of *Crépuscule with Nellie*)
Coming from Harlem to cook every day.

The Man I Love, Misterioso, Sweet'n'Lovely, Monk's Dream
– The best place to listen and brood is at home.
Sweet melodies parodied, wonderingly bent.
He longs to believe in the sweetness – but can't.
Odd pauses – then more tart notes come.

HAPPY HOUR

A neighbour arrives uninvited
to fix my eyesore garden gate.
'No sweat,' he insists.
With a young son he sends for a Coke.
'Not that I'm thirsty. I'm *training him.*'

It proceeds – though the tools aren't right.
He left his original kit with a mate
who sold the lot for forty quid.
This was before he 'understood the working class'.

Coke arrives – in a huge silver tankard.
To Andrew from all at The Bull.

Four years dry, he explains
now all diligence
barking for tools like a surgeon.
I hand them across.

Afterwards *he* invites *me* for a drink.
Dingy home . . . a grim wife . . .
but his drink range would do a Rio nightclub proud
– *Kahlua, Curaçao, Galliano, Punt e Mes*
a cupboardful of the warm south promising ease.

Take me south to the non-judgemental sun!

A strong drink ... a weak breeze ...
the little waves riding home evenly spaced
to die in rich creamy swathes on the sand ...

No – flights are fully booked.
Morons in leisurewear choke the departure lounge.
Love, take my hand.

Double duvets alone offer comfort and warmth.
We can no more fly south to be free in the sun
than return to warm our bones at the ancestral hearth.

Andrew refills with Coke.
I'm on *Crème de Banane*.

Bus conducting just now, he has plans.
(Engineering's his 'real thing', he claims.)
Take containers ... they're *everywhere*, right?
Someone has to repaint them ... *right?*
He is no naive optimist though.
'The problem is getting a yard.'

Where to locate the dream – always the catch.
Even his drink isn't properly housed.
If he still had his tools he would build
the right shrine – a crescent-moon cocktail bar
him behind, worldly and suave, serving *Genever*
Liquore Strega, *Kirsch* and *Calvados de Lachenaie* ...

Four the handmaidens with sweet-scented veils
– Alcohol, Intercourse, Stupidity, Sleep
(only one maiden a servant for life).

Sweet as thrush after rain

is the music of ice in the glass at weekends
– but tomorrow's a work day
Zen Master of evening the morning wage slave.
Out of the freezer and into the microwave.

Andrew has covered this too
and built his own alarm clock
– a monstrosity, bristling with wires
. . . like a homemade bomb.

'Demo?' he grins – but the wife intervenes
a non-drinker, now banning the clock
her face bleached as a sheep skull above the tideline
sick of crazy talk, tired in the bone
wanting neither drugged dreams nor wild bells
just the long peaceful natural sleep of her time.

SITTING WITH KAVANAGH BY THE GRAND CANAL

Where Kavanagh concealed his money under the carpet in
                                        different heaps
Displaying an intuitive understanding of the portfolio concept of
                                                spreading risk
And burned the bulk of *Kavanagh's Weekly* to boost the value of the rest
A *Certified Public Accountant* T.F. Corcoran is now upstairs
Barry & Company Auditors Accountants Financial Advisers underneath

The money men have taken his Pembrokeshire but Kavanagh does
                                        not accept defeat
Along Pembroke Road by the Grand Canal he has moved in again
                                                rent-free
A bronze man on his own bronze seat his bronze hat next to him
                                        on the seat
(For now he need never fear his comb-over blowing loose in
                                        the breeze)
Lying back arms and legs calmly crossed though somehow not
                                        at peace
Apparently not content to wallow in the habitual the banal
Looking neither left nor right at the tattooed torsoes swigging
                                        Bulmers
Or the bevy of fastidious bank girls finishing low-fat yoghurts
(Contemporary Ireland land of contrasts what would the *Weekly*
                                        have made of it all)
But focusing on somewhere in space between the somnolent canal
And *The Bank of Ireland Training Centre* on the opposite side

98

The celebrated celebrant or someone in flight from a row with
                                                    a spouse
No of course it's not pique . . . he's *composing* . . . the guy is *in thrall*
                                                    to the Muse

Citizens this is how a poet serves the gaiety of language
Staring fixedly at nothing with a furious grimace

Either that or he's pondering what to back in the first race
(The newspaper stuck in his pocket is probably turned to the
                                                    sports page)

Anyway ICI be praised for granting him this eternal rest
The pride of the standing army of poets on his own seat at last
And with room next to him circumspectly I sit and peek over
The shirt is of course open-necked both his shoes are untied
In the cradle his folded arms make with his chest
A half inch of brown liquid rain Jameson tea
Or the vial of priceless elixir he managed to snatch from the
                                                    sacred stream

Master if I drank would I be blessed and reconciled
Reading you is not enough I've never taken your advice
A hopeless addict of volition I've never wed myself to life
The way the acquiescent water takes its man-made line

Let the discontent and restlessness be purged from my soul
Instruct me in the way of the bench not the road
That the seeking is fruitless that happiness can't be pursued
(Any more than the originality and sincerity you possessed)
That you find the desiderata only when after something else

No reply and the closed lock is silent today no niagarous roar
But a used condom is ceremonially laid on a stone

And the waters of the MAXOL carwash are pouring redemption for
someone's Ford

Every man for himself symbolwise and how could my heart
not revive
With the teacher of acceptance and regeneration at my side

Though a passing youth accuses me of boring you stiff
Let me linger on a moment master of praise and rebirth
Plenipotentiary of the quotidian epicurean of ordinariness

Here beneath the blank façade of *Haughey Boland Deloitte & Touche*
The true hegemony of being re-establishes its rule

Stir cunning weeds in your private air currents
Shine healing waters in the calm light of noon

No already it's almost two arise tardy wage slaves
Go bank girls vestal virgins pledged to the sacred flame of the age
(A rapt father once in pride and awe *She got the bank*)

REJECTION AND ACCEPTANCE IN KILBURN HIGH ROAD

Like mighty tributaries mingling with the Amazon
A confluence of iron bridges at the bottom of Shootup Hill
(Metropolitan Railway 1914) two blue the third green white and gold
Provides the most attractive pigeon sanctuary in London's northwest

I would love to be the man who redeemed the pigeon in verse
But today the attention is solicited by so much else
Like UNEEK ENTERPRISES Video Hi Fi Television and Radio Dealer
Personal Export Insurance and Travel Consultants
Though the premises seem to be crammed with clapped-out gas fires

Someone has forgotten to mention that this is the age of specialists
Someone has forgotten to explain the phenomenon of imperial
                                                        overreach
MASTER SPARKLE DRY CLEANING Keys Cut Discs Engraved Shoe
                                            Repairs While U Wait
COSMETIC EXPRESSION Perfume Hair and Skin Products Special
                                            Offer Jeans £5.99
BOBY'S HOUSE OF SAREES (KILBURN) Stainless Steelware & Books

But is extravagance like energy running down in the world
FotoFare appears to have abandoned its fabulous montage confections
Of couples in frames within frames inhabiting a glass of champagne
Or laughing through the sheet music of Love is a Many Splendoured Thing

And who of whatever persuasion would not be sorry

To discover the recent demise of *The Catholic Repository*
Its window still announcing the annual pilgrimage to *Our Lady of Knock*
(This year the theme of The National Novena is *Faith and Life*)
But now devoid of holy water fonts medals statues crosses plaques
Special prayers to St Jude and St Joseph Inspirational Notelets
                                                    (Assorted)
The Irish Penal Rosary (as used in the periods of religious oppression)
And those incredible two-in-one pictures that change with your
                                                    angle of vision
The face from the Shroud of Turin alternating with the face on
                                                    the cross

Endless my lust for grotesquerie endless the urge to mock and scoff
Perpetual compulsive joking hiding the Puritan fear beneath
Seconds out for Round Ten of my quarrel with myself

Pilgrims I'd love to have faith attend a concelebrated Mass in
                                                    the Basilica
And walk in Candlelight Procession to Benediction at the Shrine

Instead it's the Sorting Office in Coventry Close
Where I go for rejected novels that always return when I'm not home

Silent swift signature then the Jiffy bag out to the street
For a close textual analysis of the three-line note
A surfeit of non-agented material . . . does not suit our list at this time

Quiet cul-de-sac luckily two unique buildings to meditate on
One appears to be a church made of corrugated iron
But displaying two boards SEA CADETS CORPS and WARNING HAZCHEM
Then THE ANIMALS' WAR MEMORIAL DISPENSARY foursquare and plain
Dedicated to the countless thousands of God's humble creatures
Who suffered grievously and perished during two World Wars
Looking forward to no final victory knowing nothing of the cause

Goddam it what do *we* know never mind the dumb brutes
We wouldn't recognise cause or victory if they crapped in our hats

Though we yearn to surrender volition we yearn to be chosen we
                                            yearn to serve
Now everybody wants to be a counsellor nobody knows how to live

Each to his own infinity we have to cry out at last
My legendary enthusiasms piercing perceptions and intuitions
Glories of solitude and analysis in the sunny through lounge
Coffee aroma from the kitchen over leather sofa bouquet
(But the blinds down a little so the suite won't fade)

Thronging oddities of the mind and the body as strange
Frozen heart tearless eyes skin that rages and weeps
Such a sensitive guy I need four different creams

But no desires hopes illusions fantasies dreams
Lucidity is the rapture I have permitted myself

And sometimes at night heady lawlessness
Darting to dump on a neighbour's skip
Dumping can bring back youth's criminal joy

So great a sweetness flows into the breast
When such as I cast out
Six months of technical journals unread

Lovers wanderers Zen poets seekers of truth
Remember me at night when the ghost of imminence returns
To roam your cul-de-sac with the wind and upset the sensitive trees

Though still I love the pilgrim's journey love the brazen garish day
Mid-afternoon light on the shameless tomato-red of SOFA SO SUITE

And McGovern's Bar seeking Big Girls for the Patrick Pearse
                                        Camogie Team
(Whether you're fit as a fiddle or fit to drop *give us a ring*)

But home is where the art is paintings books and the latest bounty
CDs bright with rainbow glory augmented by asterisked bonus tracks
Today I'm hot for Sonny Rollins and Ellington-Hodges' *Back to Back*

So avert the eyes no to temptation swiftly past *Our Price*
And home with the minor extravagance of a takeaway from
                                        The Art of Food
Aglow with reconciliation acceptance faith and gratitude
For the major innovations of London sandwich bars in our time
Crispy bacon and avocado roast duck with plum sauce
Chicken tikka on granary served by a waitress who shrieks
I've only one pair of hands and I'm using all six

Heine sing it gaily truly better a nobody in Kilburn
Than the noblest Prince of Shadows on the banks of the Styx

Better a passive surviving consumer
Than the mightiest half-God in Homer

Manifold splendours of common day and the same old jive
To you I yield at last my fastidious soul

WOMEN OF FORTY
For Martina

The imperfect is our paradise
        WALLACE STEVENS

Troubled women of forty, regretting youth, fearing the future
Despairing in front of the mirror, not you
But your ideal is false. What you lack is not perfection but faith.
Let me name the flaws – *yes!* To enumerate is an act
Of devotion and love. This imperfect is *my* paradise:
Your tough soles and toes slightly deformed by tight shoes
Startling rasp of shaved shins, roughened knees, heavy thighs
Broad commanding full moon of the buttocks with craters of
                                        cellulitis dents
(But never the Marsh of Epidemics – Sea of Serenity, Bay of Dew)
Rounded slightly protuberant belly on which I could say a High Mass
Blessing silver striations of stretch marks like skate tracks on ice
Solid thick waist (wasp waist seems a kind of *deformity* now)
Lax warm freight of breasts, curtain fold of slack flesh
At the top of the arm, underneath, where it meets the moist grove
That should never be pruned (supportive guy in most ways, I'm
Autocratic as Suleiman the Magnificent on the issue of trimming
                                        body hair)
Poignancy of worn hands (who'd have thought that *hands* aged?)
Dark lines etched on fingers, harsh so much you have grasped
Flecks of grey, face so rich in perspective, three people in one
Yourself now, the young girl you have been, the old woman to come

Fine vertical hatching on upper lip, horizontal lines on the neck
Diagonal spokes from the eyes. And so much in your deepening eyes
– Knowledge, yearning, disappointment, years of putting up

> with things

Bitter traumas with children and men, especially charming

> romantic men

The soft lute-strumming fingers becoming a fist. O my angels
At last you are ready for me – classic, rigorous, dry and austere
As Jacob's Rich Water Biscuits in their tasteful dark pack!
Turn on me your eyes asking so little, containing so much
Precisely opposite to youth (your grail and doom, blind fools).
Imagine leaving Katy Durado for vapid Grace in *High Noon*.
Katy sensual, proud, independent – *superb*. Ah Katy, don't sell up
And ride away. Take off your hat. I want to have your child.
And Jean Arthur, the wife who loved Shane but could never

> speak out

(Though he wanted her too). *Shane! Shane! I love you, Shane!*

> *Come back!*

The boy's cry was the unuttered cry in his mom's hidden heart
Silent, fixing the supper, no sob stuff there. I too loved golden Shane
But now it's Jean I see. That scene where Alan Ladd's out in the rain
Gazing in. They look and look. She is stong. It is not to be.
Katy, Jean, all my angels, it has always been thirty-five to crazy

> for me.

I never loved the young girls, enormous fun though they were.
They were beautiful but ridiculous like fastidious high-stepping birds.
The delusions, the imperious desires and demands! But, women

> of forty

I go down on my knees on the shagpile and sob with wonder

> and gratitude

For your lack of illusions and grasp of reality, you devastatingly real
With the sweet imperfections insane women pay to have

> surgeons remove.

It's our flaws make us real – and reality alone is generous.

106

The tremendous solidity and heft of the mature accommodating ass
And the cunt as wide and comfortable as a gardening hat
Which you dispose without coyness or sheet theatre
Authentic, silent as Valentino, concentrating on your pleasure
In the act I would like . . . no, forgive me, I take that back.
Your sweet marks are time's warning signs – *value, pledge, serve.*
I want to discuss ageing parents and children's careers
Your mastitis, cystitis, dysplasia, thrush, tilted womb
(Splendid name for a Women's Alternative Cabaret Group)
I want to scour shops for live yoghurt and *apply it myself*
(A tinch of organic cider vinegar in tepid water also helps)
Phone in to your boss, my voice husky with love and concern
Shop with you for new nighties and carry the heartrending
Little light case when it's time to book in for your D & C
After, nobly refrain . . . even *months* – make, instead of pleas
Avocado-stuffed rainbow trout and monkfish *à la Portugaise.*
Above all I want to splash *Veuve du Vernay* when the tests come back
Clear and, the vault of a mighty cathedral, grey sullen day
Rings with the great hymn of praise – *It's all right.*
Once again bitterness our bitter foe foiled! It may win in the end
But not yet. Raise your glass in your lovely worn hand.
Bracelets clash, shining rings vie with wine for the last of the light.
Soon the exquisite first taste that percolates slowly right down.
For those who've been warned and have heeded the warnings
A secret stupendous reward, O my angels – *everything is real.*

THE FATHER'S PRAYER
For Jane

Imagine an old pot, cluttered, grimed, forgotten on the shelf
That is taken down and flushed and filled with freshly-cut flowers.
This is something like how the birth of a daughter felt.

How we need to be dragged out into life!
Come to waken me again in my burrow
With your clear and peremptory call.

And why do I say I've got nothing done?
Already you're grown, already it's time for the father's prayer
That old and brief but heartfelt sigh – *beware.*

For besides these private words I utter public ones as well.
O confident hypocrisy of adulthood!
Gripping the lectern firmly, staring boldly into the crowd.

And once I followed stirring words and was dismayed.
I found the liberator left a trail of broken faces
Not the masks of the strong, the tender visages of girls.